A Loaf of Bread

Rana Bitar

Published by Unsolicited Press
Portland, Oregon
www.unsolicitedpress.com

Cover Image: Enana Jacob
Cover Design: Nate Miller

Printed in the United States of America.

Attention schools and businesses: for discounted copies on large orders, please contact the publisher directly.

ISBN: 978-1-947021-75-4

Contents

Where I Am From   7

Bombed   9

A Piece of Land   11

Refugee   16

Soldier   19

Beheading   22

A Loaf of Bread   25

As I Die   27

I Say My Country   30

Life and Death   33

About the Author   35

Acknowledgments   36

A Loaf of Bread

Rana Bitar

Where I Am From

I am from the cobblestones and the seven gates.
I am from cinder and grapes.
I am from the hushed steps to school
and the jasmines, white and cool.
I am from the salt of the Mediterranean
and the stones of Palmyra.
I am from the first etched letter
and the last cry of a war.

I am from the pencils in my father's drawer:
sharpened, waiting for the little fingers.
I am from the secret service boots.
I am from the attic's withered yellow-paged books.
I am from makeshift dolls and mended dresses;
from smile to the camera and make believe.
I am from the worn-out bike and the Mancala
        game.
I am from fig, wheat,
and the songs of the vendors in the street.

I am from the gurgling hookahs
and the kisses thrown from balconies.
Turkish delights and coffee's whiff.
I am from the sunrise rooster

and the sighing alleys.
I am from the flying carpet
and the magic lantern of Aladdin.

In my cabinet, there is a glued tea set;
it fell and broke one day,
beyond repair,
but I put it together again
with memories and despair.

Bombed

Silence for death
and silence for exodus.
Clamor deafens the sleeping walls
and clamor interrogates the quiet windows.

Silence for the howling
of the shuddering stones
and silence for the broken glass' groans.

My house fell—
Who will whisper lullabies to the walls' quivers?
Who will gather, kindly, the glass' scatters?
Who will search for my childhood notebooks?
Who will recall the innocent laughs?
Who will remember the elders' fables?

Who will protect my family's pictures
from the policemen's shoes?
Who will retrieve, from the garbage bins,
the curtains of my room?
Who will save the remains of my dolls
from the neighbors' snoop?

My house fell—
My father's shoes tapping on the stairs,
the house bell ringing,
the clatter of the dishes,
and the mischievous giggles.
The smell of chimney wintertime,
the breeze of summer on the balcony,
the flower pots,
and the dangling jasmine.

My house fell—
In my ears, the boom of the blow is repeated
and in my chest lies a map of fear;
I wait for its edges to fold in
so I can lay my head on it
and fall asleep.

A Piece of Land

Where do I find pain medication, my son?
I know you are busy,
baking bread
with the least amount of flour,
but the pain in my stomach
just won't stop.

Father,
you look pale,
your hands are shaking.
Let me take you to the doctor next door.

In times of war, son
do doctors care about indigestion?
They are treating gun-shot children,
reattaching fingers,
and suturing wombs.

Your skin is burning,
your pulse fast.

Father,
what is that green heaving slime?
I am sure this is more than indigestion.

We need a doctor right now.

Son,
the roads are blocked.
Bombs are being dropped,
shrapnel flying,
and snipers are waiting nearby.
I will not let you risk your life
for a bellyache.
I will not let you go out.

But, Father,
I do it all the time.
I go out,
and I am still here,
as you can see.

You go out, my son, to get food
so your children won't starve.
You go out to get jugs of water
that would last for a month's time.
You go out to cut trees for burning
so your children won't freeze.
I won't let you go out for me.

Father,
your skin is damp,

your bedsheets are wet.
Look, seeing this,
the children's eyes are twitching in fear.
You are coming with me right now!

You see, son,
I only need pain medication
—if you have—
If not, it is okay.
Do not panic.
I will be fine.

Father,
your skin is cool;
your pulse is slow.
You stopped heaving.
I call you,
and you do not respond.
Father, are you all right?

The doctor said,
"Nothing can be done.
No ambulance will make it
through the roadblocks in time."
Father,
you stopped breathing.
I think you are gone.

Father,
forgive me for breaking the rules.
There are no funeral homes to approach.
I am asking around
for a nearby burial ground.
Will you forgive me for doing that?

Father,
I know your wish had been
to be buried in your hometown.
But it is too dangerous
to travel out of this town.

Alone,
I am throwing soil on the coffin.
No one is here to say goodbye—
no ceremonies,
no speeches,
and no prayers.

Father,
I have to hurry.
I hear the snipers' bullets whizzing by.
At home, two children await.

Father, forgive me,
for we are born

to a country that denies us,
at the end,
a piece of land
to call a burial ground.

Refugee

Do you know my name?
Can you roll
its heavy letters on your tongue?
I've been excavated,
tumbled,
chased,
and thrown.
I have no flag, I float.
I push towards shore.
Rationed UN rice and bread await.
A small gas oven will heat my tent
and mute my lonely wail.
I float.

I float
in the hollow eyes
of my hungry children--
detached
and alone.
I float.
I do not belong.
The corners I long to moor
wave from a distance,
then abort my throws.

I float
in my empty pockets—
a speck of dust
in a ray of light
flutters in place.
Pushes, pushes, but it doesn't go—
only floats, and floats, and floats.

I float
on the quiet numbness
of my soul—
leveled rebels of history
and my home.
The world outside
runs around
from a little puddle
to another--
splashes to make a noise,
churns bubbles to make a scene.
All that I hear
is deafness.
All that I see
is emptiness.
I close my eyes,
sail away,
push and push,

but I don't reach.

And I decide,
maybe, it is wise
to inhabit my anger,
throw myself in the lair,
be smitten by the roar,
let it rip my heart,
let it devour my eyes.

Maybe, if these beats stop,
my heart would turn to a stone.
Maybe, if these eyes die,
my tears would become a tomb.
Maybe, if I smother my wings,
my soul would just walk away
and never look back again.

Soldier

Mother,
forgive me,
I will not be coming back.
I went to fetch a jug of water
from the government's ration van.
I was stopped.
I was told
that I was old enough
to carry arms,
old enough to stand up
and fight for my country—
for my fellow countrymen.

They handed me a machine gun,
heavier than I am.
They said,
"You do not even have to aim.
Close your eyes
and let the machine claim the scene."
They said
I am old enough to feel proud
of my ability to spill blood.
They said
I will get used to it—

severing heads and all the rest.

Mother,
they may be right.
I do not know.
I know they said that
I could not refuse.
They asked me if I would prefer
to see my blood
or someone else's spilled today.
I said,
"No, not mine.
My mother is sick and alone."
They said
that you would be proud to know
that I did not come back home
to you in time because
I am a soldier now.

They said
that you would not like it
if one of them came to you,
instead of me,
with a plastic bag.
In it,
you would see my body,
separated from my head,

for you to mourn
before you're shot dead.

Mother,
I don't know
how many men and children
I will kill.
I will always close my eyes.
I will not aim.
This machine is heavy on me,
but I guess it will protect me.
I don't know
what else they're going to ask me to do.
But I will have to do it
with my eyes shut
and my soul closed.

And maybe,
if I cannot bear the pain,
I will stand
in front of somebody else's
machine gun.

Forgive me, mother—
your son has been turned
into a soldier.

Beheading

Mother,
my knees are dug
into the sand.
In a few mutters,
my head will brush the ground.
This muddy grave
will feed on my limbs
and only an orange shroud
will be left behind.
The sand will cough,
shake off the howl of my blood,
and dry up its grains
to host other knees to come.

Mother,
these black masks
are eager to preside
over the pulse of my veins
and suck,
from my lungs,
the tangles of air.

Mother,
mouth is parched,

pulse is dragging,
numbed beats are fleeting.
Fear is a luxury—
an excess
to a resolved mind.

Mother,
the blade is dusty and cold.
I remember when I was a child
I threw a tantrum once—
my throat was tight
and my voice was clogged.
It feels the same now
except today,
there will be no other concessions to make,
there will be no other breath to take.

Mother,
the last pulsating thought in my panting brain
is your tears—
diamonds commingled
with crimson' seep.
                    Do not watch
                         Do not watch.
Take me in your arms.
Rock me to sleep,
your little baby boy.

Only in your arms
will love defeat
death.

A Loaf of Bread

There is a promise
of flour and bread.
Mother,
wait--
I want to fulfill it.

Mother,
finally,
we are going to eat
something
other than stones today.

Mother,
what is going on?
The loaf of bread's face
has morphed
into an airplane,
a shower of shrapnel
has studded my body,
and the neighborhood's bakery
has become my holocaust.

Mother,
some of them are hungrier

than we are.
They waited in line
to snipe the life
left in us.
They spread the asphalt—
a table.
Our remains on it,
scattered—
a feast.

Mother,
it seems there is still some life
left in me.
I see half of my body
a few steps away
from my head.

Mother,
this injury does not hurt.
But a heaviness
inhabits my heart
when I see
my neighbor's mouth
and my friend's guts
splattered on the sidewalk—
bloodied, yet they are
still hungry.

As I Die

(Alone, And in a Country at War)

In my country,
they stole my identity card
and snipped my rosary.
They robbed me
as I closed my eyes
to sleep through
my loneliness.
What peace is waiting for me in my grave?
What disappointment is fencing my cemetery?

I asked the gravedigger
to recite the names of my brothers,
the names of their wives,
and the names of their children.
I asked him to dig deeper
so I can bury my memories.

The jasmine in my garden
is calling me:
with the smell of summer that was assassinated,
the merchants' calls that disappeared,
the flowers' syrup that turned sour,

the coffee cups that were shattered
with what, once upon a time, was--
but, after today, will never be again.

In my country,
there will be no flowers
to top my coffin—
only my shame
will embellish my grave.

Lonely,
I don't dare to think
and I don't dare to remember.
Lonely,
I don't dare to ask.
Today,
I vanish in the darkness,
stripped—
even from my own identity.
Who, tomorrow, will find my cross?
Who will locate my rosary?

They divided, like thieves,
my remains.
Children—I gave them, at Easter time,
olive branches to hold.
Neighbors—I greeted them

when they stopped by my garden
to clip a flower
or smell a rose.

I asked the gravedigger
to recite the names of my brothers,
the names of their wives,
and the names of their children.
I asked him that if,
one day, someone finds
my identity card,
to wipe off my grave
the dust of shame.

I call on you, my country,
you who expelled my loved ones:
before you bury me,
you ought to bury, in the darkness,
my sorrows and my regrets.
You ought to make me forget
my family's faces.
You ought to let the dust wash out
my desolation.

I Say My Country

I say my country—
and the giddiness of the jasmines' white is,
in the red grief,
drowning.

I say my country—
and the warm memory of the place,
whenever I recall it,
vomits in my face.

I say my country—
and I search the fog
for a placenta
or an umbilical cord,
but I stumble upon
a guillotine and
a gallows' rope.

I say my country—
and I refuse to replace "*Bab El Hara* *"
with the dismembered body parts.
I refuse to replace
discussing a vote for *"Star Academy* *"*
with discussing conspiracy theories.

I say my country—
and my alliance sobs,
lost in the fog
of biddings and mobs.

To whom I belong?
To a cold shadow in the pastors' clothes?
To a hibernation, hidden in the wood of a cross?
To a turbulence, living in the Quran's pages?
To a torrent of anger, sweating the blood of
resentful rage?
To a holocaust that burns all religions and faiths?
To a scream of madness, calling for Nero's flames?

To whom I belong?
To a death, assuming the children's forms?
To a bomb's fragments, disintegrating in my
womb,
and in the head of my killers?
To a butcher that had become your neighbor
and my neighbor?
And who recognizes the identity of this hung meat?
And who still has, in their eyes,
one tear instead of a stone?

I say my country—
and I dismount the steed in my fairytale.

I fasten its straps to the gate of pain.
I wait for the flood
and I pray that I see the light of dawn—
in my days.

*Two of the most watched Arabic TV show series.

Life and Death

Let's make love
while death is being made somewhere else.
The only way to know you are alive
is to hear your heartbeats scream—
to make your senses soar to an extreme.
Because the opposite of death is not life.
The opposite of death is love.

About the Author

Rana Bitar earned her master's degree in English and Creative Writing from Southern New Hampshire University in January 2017. Her poetry appeared in *The Deadly Writers Patrol journal, DoveTales journal, Earthen Lamp Journal, Magnolia Review, Pittsburgh Poetry Review*, and *El Portal journal*.

Professionally, she is a physician. She lives and works in upstate NY. She is currently working on a collection of creative nonfiction stories about her journey as an oncologist. She writes both in Arabic and English.

Acknowledgments

A Loaf of Bread appeared in *The Deadly Writers Patrol*, fall issue, 2016.

As I Die appeared in *The Deadly Writers Patrol*, fall issue, 2016, and in *DoveTales*, May 2017 issue.

Bombed appeared in *DoveTales*, May 2017 issue.

Refugee appeared in *DoveTales*, May 2017 issue.

32776501R00024

Made in the USA
Lexington, KY
06 March 2019